GALAXY OF SUPERSTARS

Ben Affleck

Backstreet Boys

Brandy

Garth Brooks

Mariah Carey

Matt Damon

Cameron Diaz

Leonardo DiCaprio

Céline Dion

Tom Hanks

Hanson

Jennifer Love Hewitt

Lauryn Hill

Jennifer Lopez

Ricky Martin

Ewan McGregor

Mike Myers

'N Sync

LeAnn Rimes

Adam Sandler

Britney Spears

Spice Girls

Jonathan Taylor Thomas

Venus Williams

CHELSEA HOUSE PUBLISHERS

GALAXY OF SUPERSTARS

Ricky Martin

Matthew Newman

CHELSEA HOUSE PUBLISHERS
Philadelphia

Frontis: *Performing in concert, Ricky Martin, the hottest new Latino superstar, radiates the energy and power that have thrilled fans around the world.*

Produced by
21st Century Publishing and Communications, Inc.
New York, New York
http://www.21cpc.com

CHELSEA HOUSE PUBLISHERS

Editor in Chief: Stephen Reginald
Managing Editor: James D. Gallagher
Production Manager: Pamela Loos
Art Director: Sara Davis
Director of Photography: Judy L. Hasday
Senior Production Editor: J. Christopher Higgins
Publishing Coordinator/Project Editor: James McAvoy

The Chelsea House World Wide Web address is
http://www.chelseahouse.com

First Printing

1 3 5 7 9 8 6 4 2

Library of Congress Cataloging-in-Publication Data

Newman, Matthew.
   Ricky Martin / by Matthew Newman.
      p. cm. — (Galaxy of superstars)
   Includes bibliographical references (p. 62) and index.
   Summary: Profiles the life and career of the Latin pop star best known for his hit song "Livin' la Vida Loca."
ISBN 0-7910-5771-2 (hc) — ISBN 0-7910-5772-0 (pbk.)
   1. Martin, Ricky—Juvenile literature. 2. Singers —Latin America—Biography—Juvenile literature. [1. Martin, Ricky. 2. Singers. 3. Puerto Ricans—Biography.]
I. Title. II. Series.

ML3930.M328 N48 2000
782.42164'092—dc21
[B]   99-462030
                                                                      CIP
                                                                       AC

Contents

Chapter 1
Ricky Rocks the Grammys!   7

Chapter 2
The Bubblegum Kings   17

Chapter 3
Getting out of the Fast Lane   25

Chapter 4
The Hospital Heartthrob   35

Chapter 5
Lighting up Broadway   39

Chapter 6
The Cup Runneth Over   47

Chapter 7
Livin' la Vida Loca   53

Chronology   60
Accomplishments   61
Further Reading   62
Index   64

1

RICKY ROCKS
THE GRAMMYS!

It was all in those *amazing* hips. In Los Angeles, California, on February 24, 1999, Ricky Martin woke up the Grammy Awards with an electrifying musical performance—and a sizzling, swiveling hip action that viewers had not seen since Elvis Presley. On that night, the Ricky Martin "explosion" began across America.

Today, Ricky Martin seems to be everywhere. His image graces the cover of *Time* magazine; he appears at the MTV Music Awards and on his own television special. When, in July 1999, Ricky announced an American concert tour, the event sold out in minutes in cities around the country. Indeed, this hot young star has redefined the standard of success for a crossover artist. His trademark Spanglish phrase—"Livin' la Vida Loca" ("Living the Crazy Life") is now part of America's vocabulary. In an especially flattering measure of fame, many teens have adopted the Ricky Martin look, hair in a buzz cut with a touch of blond highlights in the front.

Ricky is not an overnight sensation, however. Before his appearance at the Grammys, he had been performing

---

The audience at the 1999 Grammy Awards in Los Angeles came alive when Ricky Martin broke into his signature song, "La Copa de la Vida," and rocked the arena. Ricky's performance marked his breakthrough from Latino star into superstar of the pop music scene.

Following his Grammy performance, Ricky showed no signs of slowing down. He toured, recorded, and was in demand for television talk shows. On The Oprah Winfrey Show, *he appeared with host Winfrey (right) and fellow Latina star Jennifer Lopez (center).*

for 15 years and had already sold 13 million albums, first as a member of the teen band Menudo and then as a solo Latin artist. Much of Ricky's appeal comes from his brilliant mixture of sounds. His music is Latin, yet pop, skat, yet retro, romantic but also with a definite edge.

Ricky's rise to the top really accelerated following his performance on the Grammys. "For me, it was yesterday," Ricky told *Rolling Stone.* "But instead of grabbing America by storm, America caught me. Ever since [the Grammys], I've been living, literally, la vida loca—the crazy life. Although I must admit I've been in a spin for the last two years—since I started working on the crossover from the Latin market to Europe and then Asia."

The song that rocked the Grammys was "La Copa de la Vida" ("The Cup of Life"), the official soccer anthem that Ricky had performed in 1998 at the World Cup championship in France—in front of a billion television viewers. This was the performance that caught the eye of the Grammy show producers. In the words of *Time* magazine, "He had done the impossible. He had sung about soccer in Spanish and got Americans to care."

On the night of the Grammys, a lot was riding on how well Ricky's performance would be received. In many Latin countries, as well as in Asia and Europe, his music was already very popular, but now he was facing the toughest audience of all—his peers in America. Since his early "bubblegum" days in Menudo, Ricky had struggled to achieve true artistic recognition. The young singer was also on the verge of releasing his first album in English, and he was anxious for it to do well in the United States.

Arriving at the Grammys, Ricky knew his musical future depended a great deal on his performance that night. Once inside the auditorium, he mingled with such musical stars as Will Smith, Céline Dion, and Sting. The "established" Latin contingent was also there, including Gloria Estefan and Jon Secada, as well as the "new" Latin wave, represented by such artists as Colombian rock singer Shakira, New York salsa singer Marc Anthony, and Ricky's soon-to-be Top 40 companion, singer and actress Jennifer Lopez.

Accompanying Ricky at the Grammys was a group of his closest friends, among them Robi Draco Rosa, one of the producers of "Livin' la Vida Loca" and a former bandmate in Menudo. Other friends included Emilio Estefan (husband of Gloria) and Desmond Child, one of the songwriters on Ricky's first

English-language album (still to be released at that time). Ricky was also accompanied by a tall blonde beauty named Rebecca de Alba, who was his girlfriend at that time.

As usual, Ricky was dressed to kill in black leather pants and a sleek, long-sleeved shirt, and his 1,000-watt smile radiated confidence. Still, somewhere between the screams of the adoring fans outside and the "been there, done that" stare of the audience, inside, Ricky was feeling tested.

To calm himself, he practiced yoga inside his dressing room. "I was so anxious at the Grammys," Ricky reported later. "So I said, 'Dude, you've been doing this for 15 years. Just be yourself.' Then I went, 'Hey, Sting, you know what?'" Then Ricky gave Sting a little preview of his hip action. "Check this out, bro'. I knew he'd remember me."

Finally, an hour and 20 minutes into the show, the Grammys' host, Rosie O'Donnell, introduced Ricky. When Ricky unleashed his parade of performers, the audience suddenly came alive as the beat of "La Copa de la Vida" thundered through the auditorium. Congo players, women on stilts, and dancers thronged the aisles while people leaped up to dance to the drumbeats.

As excitement grew, dancers appeared at center stage and deposited a mysterious silver box. While viewers stared curiously, Ricky sprang from the box and took over the stage. "Do you really want it?" he shouted. Fans rushed toward the stage; ribbons, balloons, and streamers flew around the hall. As the music rose to a crescendo, Ricky jumped to the top of a staircase.

Everyone was watching those hips.

"I love to do hips," Ricky confessed to *TV Guide*. "But let's be honest, that goes back to my culture. When you dance salsa, or samba, it's all in the hips."

Ricky's stunning performance of "La Copa de la Vida" was followed by a wild ovation. Throwing out kisses, he glistened in the warm embrace of the audience, savoring the moment. As Latino television star Jimmy Smits said later, "Ricky rocked the house!"

Backstage after his performance, Ricky knew his nerves would be tested yet again that night. He had been nominated for a Grammy for Best Latin Pop Performance, and he was competing with such famous musical artists as Jose Feliciano and Enrique Iglesias. It would be a true test of whether the music world really accepted him for his art or simply saw him as a passing fad. It was common knowledge that not all Grammy voters appreciated modern music styles, and other hip, nontraditional Latin performers had been shunned by the decision makers in prior years.

At this moment in his career, Ricky was in the forefront of a Latin crossover crusade. As he told *Time* magazine:

> A lot of people say, well why English? Why do you want to do it in the states? It's all about communicating. The last album, *Vuelve* ["Come Back"], did really good, to be quite honest—I want to be humble about this—all over the world. One of the songs was number one in 22 countries. And it was in Spanish. So I didn't have to go to English to make it.

But make no mistake. Ricky definitely wanted to succeed in the United States, and when his name was announced as a Grammy winner, he was truly excited. "I have a Grammy," the grateful winner said emotionally. Afterwards, he made a special point of thanking the Grammy voters for giving Latin music the attention it deserves.

While Ricky addressed the press backstage, fellow Grammy winner Madonna came up from behind to hug him, exclaiming, "I'm just here to congratulate him! All I can say is, 'Watch out!' I had to sneak up on him. He's so cute!" Like everyone else from the show business industry who was present and felt the buzz that evening, Madonna recognized a hot trend coming when she saw one.

After the night of the Grammys, "the crazy life" really began for Ricky. Sales of his album *Vuelve* increased 400 percent. He cut a new album which featured a duet with Madonna, "Be Careful with My Heart," and followed up with the release in May of his new video, *Livin' la Vida Loca.*

These days, the flame is still burning very hot, but Ricky has no intention of becoming a mere flash-in-the-pan. His goal is to make Spanish music even more popular and to gain increased awareness and respect for Latin music.

For Ricky, who speaks five languages fluently—Spanish, Portuguese, English, Italian, and French—it is important that his Spanish-speaking fans understand why he released an album in English after years of only producing Spanish-language music.

He is not abandoning his Latin fans but rather is bringing Latin sounds to his new productions and audiences as he increases awareness and broadens his fan base. Based

on the enthusiastic reception Ricky receives everywhere he goes and the energy and passion he brings to his music, it is not Ricky who is changing, only the language in which he sings.

Ricky certainly wants success, but he also admits that he wants it on his own terms. Determined to be more than a bubblegum heartthrob, he has worked extremely hard to

Not only did Ricky perform at the Grammys, he also won the award for Best Latin Pop Performance for his album Vuelve. *With this trophy, Ricky proved that he was truly among the new generation of Latino stars.*

Ricky shares the Grammy spotlight with Madonna, who enthused over his performance. Following the Grammys, the two recorded the duet "Be Careful with My Heart" for Ricky's English-language album Ricky Martin.

reach his goal, and he has no intention of compromising his personal artistic vision. One of the reasons Ricky respects artists like Madonna so much is because they have risen above the status of being mere sex symbols. As producer Robi Rosa said in *People* magazine, "Sex appeal is equal to no appeal. He is into touching a lot of hearts."

When asked about his Grammy Award, Ricky told *Entertainment Tonight*:

> For me to win a Grammy is having to grow more. This is my priority every day, to learn something before I go to bed. . . . I'm going to do this for a long time, so if I receive a Grammy, I'm definitely going to be surrounded by more talented people. I'm just going to keep pushing myself.

Along with being humble, Ricky is also committed to using all the tools he has at his disposal—including those amazing hips. "To see Will Smith doing the jiggy with my song . . . it's overwhelming," Ricky commented.

2

THE BUBBLEGUM KINGS

I magine this scenario: Every night you perform in front of thousands of goo-goo eyed girls, all panting for your attention. You are the lead singer in the first Spanish-language teen band to enjoy true crossover success in America. All eyes are upon you every night as you whirl and croon before an adoring audience.

During your first month with the band, you play 10 sold-out shows for 200,000 fans at Radio City Music Hall in New York City. After the shows, you are whisked away in a limo back to the hotel. With visions of the Beatles in your head, you push your way through a mob of fans outside your hotel, some screaming your name, some seeking an autograph, others just wanting a glimpse of your face.

As you tour internationally, the world is your playground. You never have to pay for a meal, and everything in your life is taken care of—there are no chores, no sharing your room with a sibling, no part-time job at McDonald's to help make ends meet. Your hotel room is

Ricky's roots are in Puerto Rico, the lush tropical island where he was born. As a child, he knew he wanted to be a performer, and he began his career with the boy band Menudo. A mere month after signing with the band, he was entertaining audiences at New York City's Radio City Music Hall.

your school. Every day, you enjoy new and exciting things: giving interviews, recording in studios, and appearing on television.

If you should ever get lonely, you can pour over mounds of fan letters, and fans are always waiting outside your door if you should choose to meet them.

One more thing: You are only 13 years old.

Such was the life for young Ricky Martin as a member of Menudo. In commenting about this period with the band, he said that "It was like Disneyland."

Long before Ricky Martin was a solo international pop star, he was part of another incredible pop phenomenon, the band Menudo. In Spanish, the name means "small," but the success of the band was anything but small. Menudo was a hugely successful "boy band" that was originally formed in 1977 and which exists to this day.

Over the course of Ricky's five years in Menudo, the band visited Japan, Guam, Spain, Brazil (singing in Portuguese), the Philippines (singing in English), and Latin America (singing in Spanish).

At the height of Menudo's fame, the band had its own Saturday morning television show, starred in a feature film, and even sold its own dolls in toy stores. In an appropriately quirky career statement, Ricky and the other four members of Menudo once made a celebrity appearance on the television show *The Love Boat*. Outside the United States, weekly Menudo TV specials were broadcast in Latin America, and multilingual albums were produced in English, Spanish, Portuguese, Tagalog (Philippine), and Italian.

In spite of Menudo's teenybopper glory, the

band had one fatal flaw—in reality, it wasn't a band at all. Menudo treated all its members as if they were interchangeable parts, the idea being that the members stay forever young to reflect the look and feel of teenagers. All the boys had to be under 16 and from Puerto Rico. Each member could only stay in the group until he was 18, at which time he was rotated out of the band and replaced by another member.

For Ricky, joining Menudo was a chance to do many of the things he had always dreamed about: singing, dancing, performing onstage, recording, traveling the world, and meeting girls. For a young Puerto Rican boy, Menudo represented the hottest game in town and a ticket to the international stage.

Born Enrique Martin Morales on Christmas Eve in 1971 in San Juan, Puerto Rico, Ricky is the youngest child of Enrique Martin, his namesake, and Nereida Morales. The only child of his parents, who were divorced when he was three, his family includes four stepbrothers—Erick, Daniel, Angel, Fernando—and one step-sister, Vanessa. To this day, Ricky is very close to his family. One of his brothers is his stage manager, and the others also travel with him.

Ricky's mother and father remained friends after their divorce, and Ricky, who lived near them both, moved happily back and forth between them and also stayed with his maternal grandparents. As he recalled, "I never had to make decisions about who I loved more. I was always happy."

Early on, Ricky knew that a career as a performer was his destiny. As he told *People in Español:* "I would gather the neighbors and do plays on the street with my friends."

Recognizing his son's potential, Ricky's

father went looking for an agent and found a modeling agency in a mall. As Ricky remembers, "I stood in front of a camera; they took pictures and said, 'What's your name?'"

"Kiki," Ricky replied, remembering a nickname his grandmother had given him. "After that," he explained, "I did 30 commercials in 3 years—sodas, toothpaste, any commercial you could do from age seven to ten."

By age 11, Ricky had landed Burger King and Orange Crush commercials, among others. As a student in Catholic school, he also sang in the choir and performed in school plays. "He was cast each time he went to an audition," says his father. "They told him, 'Do this,' and he would do it. He had an incredible ability."

Ricky had big dreams from the beginning, but he knew the sacrifices a life in show business would entail, as he told *MTV News*:

> When I was 6 years old I told [my] dad, "I want to be an artist." He said, "Okay so how can I help you?" My father was a psychologist. My mother is an accountant. Nobody's in the music business.

Ricky recalls that his father took his request very seriously, however, telling his son:

> You know what you're saying. You know what you want. You know what comes with all this. You have to deal with the fact that maybe one day you want to be with your family [and] you're not going to be able to because there are responsibilities to take care of.

"I was only six years old, but he was trying to open my eyes a little," Ricky concluded.

As a preteen, all Ricky could think about

was getting into Menudo. "My parents were very supportive, but they weren't the typical stage parents," Ricky told *America Online*. "My first audition [for Menudo] I took my bike and I showed up. I came back home, telling my parents that I was leaving to be an entertainer. I was eleven years old at the time. They started laughing and then, they started crying. That was twelve years ago."

At the time that Ricky first auditioned to join Menudo, it was the allure of stardom rather than a love of art that motivated him. "I didn't want to be a singer. I wanted to be Menudo, I wanted to give concerts, to travel, to

Ricky (far right) sings with the boys of Menudo in a studio in New York City. Menudo was often called a "recycling factory" because its members kept rotating. Once a member reached 18, he was considered too old and was forced out of the group.

meet the girls. I had been a fan of the group that began in 1977. I was always stubborn and determined to be one of them."

For his initial audition, Ricky presented much of what Menudo was looking for: good looks, a decent voice, and excellent dance moves. He was rejected, however, because he was too short. At age 12, he was undersized; as an adult, Ricky stands at 6' 2". The young hopeful tried again, this time with cowboy boots to add to his perceived height. Once more he was rejected.

Ricky would not give up, and as it turned out, his third attempt was charmed. He was accepted into the band and became the youngest member at the time. Once Ricky joined Menudo in 1984, the manager made Ricky's mission quite clear. Never mind "art," he was told. The goal was: make the girls swoon, wear the clothes and the hairstyle we tell you to, and hit the marks every night onstage.

"He was small, not a big singer, and his voice was not so good then," the group's manager at the time, Edgardo Diaz, later reported. "But we thought he could learn a lot by being with the group."

It was an enormous transition for anyone, let along a young boy. Not very long after joining Menudo, little Ricky was performing onstage at Radio City Music Hall in New York City before a sold-out audience. "One day I was riding my bike in the park," he said later, "and the next I was performing in front of 200,000 people."

For Ricky, being accepted into the popular band was a dream come true, although it was not always easy being part of the demanding

"Menudo machine." His mixed emotions are quite apparent in this comment he made to *TV Guide*:

> Everything, they tell you what to do . . . [but] you were sitting under the Eiffel Tower when you were 12 years old, and kids in your classroom were reading about it. . . . Complaining is for losers.

Menudo was the first Spanish-speaking pop band to really break through in America. Although the rewards were great, so were the demands made on the members. The band toured and recorded all-year round. During Ricky's five years with the band, it produced more albums than many groups do in a lifetime, including 17 albums in five languages—an average of more than three albums a year.

For Ricky, however, the hectic schedule, being away from home for long periods, and some family tensions were taking their toll. He knew that Menudo would not be forever, and he had to make a decision.

3

GETTING OUT
OF THE FAST LANE

In the summer of 1989, Menudo's success was at its all-time high. In many countries across the globe, the band was selling millions of records, performing sold-out concert after sold-out concert to mobs of screaming fans, and making millionaires of the five boys in the band. Never mind that the band members couldn't select their own clothes, or their own hairstyles, or even choose which songs they played. For Ricky, the fast life of Menudo was a far cry from the days when he rode his bike down the streets of San Juan, listening to his rock heroes Cheap Trick and Boston, dreaming of one day performing in the United States.

In spite of the lack of personal and artistic freedom, however, it was as close to being a dream come true as a young man could imagine. Still, as he turned 18 and his tenure with the band was about to end, Ricky was unsure of how he felt. For a long time, he had been aware that being in a "concept" band had cramped his style; he wanted to do more than dress sharp and perform the same dance moves every night.

Ricky performs a solo number while on tour with Menudo. He liked the fame that came with the band, but the fast lane of touring, rehearsals, and mobs of fans was exhausting.

"Our creativity was stifled," Ricky complained to *People*. "We were told [the songs we wrote] were no good. We began to question the need for rehearsing the same routines over and over."

After five long years, Ricky started to rebel. "I wouldn't show up for interviews . . . [but] I never missed a show; I still loved being onstage. It was more, 'I'm not motivated. In fact, I'm starting to hate this,'" he recalled during a later interview.

One very important incident that stayed with Ricky reflected what he has called the "militaristic" nature of Menudo. When he was 15, he asked for time off from a tour to visit Iraida, his grandmother, who was ailing. An artist who had been influential in Ricky's life, she was the one person who was closest to Ricky in the whole world. As a boy he had spent more time with Iraida than with his own mother, and in a way it was his grandmother who brought him up and taught him to believe in himself as an artist.

Ricky's request for a break in the schedule was denied, and while he was on tour, his grandmother died. Although he still went on with his duties, he was disappointed and angry at the way he was treated. For five years he had been trained to be part of a group. He was not allowed to be an individual or to show his inner feelings. As far as the management of Menudo was concerned, he was not Ricky Martin but Ricky Menudo.

Ricky wasn't the only one feeling imprisoned within the band. His best friend, fellow Menudo member Robi Draco Rosa, was also frustrated and determined to do something about it. In the 20-odd-year history of the band, Rosa was the only member to ever leave before being asked to. Like Ricky, he too was very young, and the worldwide travel and the screaming fans were exhilarating to a young guy. Unlike Ricky, though, Rosa could not stick it out until he was 18. He quit in the middle of a tour in Brazil and wandered to Puerto Rico and Argentina, finally winding up in the United States in Los Angeles.

Afterward, Rosa started his own group, called Maggie's Dream, which toured with the Black Crows and Faith No More.

Rosa, who plays the wild retro-guitar lead on "Livin' la Vida Loca," has always been a creative mentor for Ricky. "I don't remember when we first met," Rosa has said. "It's like asking when I met one of my cousins. He's part of my family."

In fact, when they met, Rosa was 12 and Ricky was nine. For Ricky, Rosa's departure from Menuda was a wake-up call. Rosa was making the career move that Ricky really wanted to make: venturing out for something new, free to fly or crash on his own terms.

But leaving the group was much tougher for Ricky than it was for Rosa, who has commented, "Rick was the one who really loved to be in front of the crowd." In actuality, the decision to leave Menudo was already made for Ricky, based on the band's "18 and out" policy. "My last concert was in Puerto Rico, my hometown. I am a man who cries, and I cried a lot," Ricky remembered thoughtfully. After exactly five years, Ricky left the band on July 10, 1989.

For the young performer, the road ahead was unfamiliar and very uncertain. Few of the group's alumni had moved on to bigger and better careers. Going back home to Puerto Rico wasn't the easiest option either. During Ricky's time with Menudo, tensions between his mother and father had built up, as each parent wanted to be with their son when he returned home from touring. Although he loved both of his parents dearly, it was extremely difficult being in the middle of their torn friendship.

Ricky couldn't split himself in two to deal with his parents' competing requests, and he became angry at life in general. He seemed to especially resent his father, who had been instrumental in getting him started as an entertainer. Ricky later acknowledged that he was probably the problem, not his parents, as he rebelled against all the demands put on him. He was giving his energies to his career and not to his family.

Ricky also said later that he did not blame his father, but it appears that at the time he did. According to Ricky, the senior Martin "wanted me to choose between him and my mother. How do you ask a child to do that?" In anger, Ricky would not speak with his father for almost 10 years.

Ricky's anger at his father didn't solve his inner problems, however. Trying to come to terms with his future, he moved in with his mother in Puerto Rico, where for a week he thought hard about what to do next. As he later recalled, "I didn't know if I wanted to stay in the business or go back to school. One day I said, 'Mom, I'm going to New York for a vacation. I'll be back in ten days.' Never came back."

In New York City, Ricky took what was for him a radically dramatic step: After years of

having everything "handled" for him, he became responsible for running his own life. He rented an apartment, put his own food on the table, and instead of being told what to do every minute, made up his own mind about everything. In recalling that period of his life Ricky said later: "I came to New York City to do nothing. . . . You know, for me, it was fascinating to go and walk and sit on a bench in a

Tired and at odds with his family, Ricky headed for New York City, where he took a three-year break. He relaxed, took in the sights, and sat on park benches watching the people go by until a friend invited him to Mexico City.

park and look at people walk by . . ."

Being on his own in New York City brought a feeling of liberation to Ricky. He had time to think about his career and came to the realization that while being in Menudo was a great experience, that part of his life was definitely over. Some years later, in reflecting on his years with Menudo, he had some advice for young people thinking of joining a boy band. "Enjoy it," he said. "Be a sponge. It's not gonna last forever."

For three years, Ricky stayed in New York. He spent time in the parks, visited museums, worked out at the gym, and cleaned his apartment. However, he did more than just that—he also signed a record deal with Sony Records. Sony released Ricky's first album of original songs, the self-titled Spanish-language album *Ricky Martin*, in 1992, an event that launched his solo career.

That same year, in a fortunate turn of events, Ricky accepted the invitation of a friend to visit Mexico City for a weekend. It would be the longest weekend Ricky ever spent. "I flew to Mexico on Friday," he said, "went to see a play on Tuesday, and the following Monday I opened in the theatre."

In just a few days, Ricky had auditioned and was accepted for a role in the musical *Mamá Ama el Rock* ("Mom Loves Rock"). A very popular production, the show was a launching pad for Ricky's next venture—into Mexican television—where he appeared in the soap opera *Alcanzar una Estrella II* ("Reaching for a Star 2").

A story about musicians yearning for success, the soap opera was wildly popular in Mexico, and with his good looks, so was Ricky.

He soon appeared in concert, with the band from the show, as well as the other singers and actors, touring Mexico as part of the Muñecos del Papel ("Paper Dolls"). The group also went on to cut an album that sold more than a million copies.

Not long thereafter, Ricky was tapped for a role in the film *Mas que Alcanzar una Estrella* ("More Than Reaching for a Star"). For his portrayal of Pablo in the film, he won Mexico's highest acting award, the Heraldo.

At the same time, Ricky's first recording for Sony was selling well, and he launched a South American tour to promote the album. *Ricky Martin* stayed on the Latin charts for 41 weeks and ultimately sold 500,000 copies—the most ever for a debut Latin artist on the Sony label.

Cutting albums, touring, and appearing on television did not give Ricky very much time for personal relationships. He did, however, find room in his life for Rebecca de Alba, a host on Mexican television, whom he had known since his soul-searching days after leaving Menudo. Talking to one reporter about Rebecca, Ricky has said, "I dated this incredible woman. I shouldn't say 'dated', we were together, boyfriend and girlfriend, when I first moved to Mexico." When asked how they met again in Mexico, he simply explains that it was in the hallway of the building housing her television network in Mexico City. "I was on the show, and she was there." Over time, Ricky's relationship with Rebecca would prove to be one of his most enduring romantic attachments.

At age 22, with his long hair and a bare-chested rock-star persona, Ricky's image and

Ricky and his long-time girlfriend Rebecca de Alba appeared arm in arm at the Grammys in 1999. He met Rebecca when he was 18, and their relationship has endured through years of breakups and reconciliations.

sound still displayed more than just a little teenybopper appeal. His albums may not have been terrific artistic masterpieces, but his singing and acting were opening doors to his eventual success as a Latino star who would become a household name in the United States.

4

THE HOSPITAL
HEARTTHROB

Viewers who tuned into the American soap opera *General Hospital* in 1994 watched a character named Miguel Morez encounter a wild, incredible series of events, including a torrid love affair, a meeting with a mobster, and a reconciliation with a long-lost son. Ricky Martin—alias Miguel—was the newest soap opera heartthrob.

Hot on the heels of his acting success in Mexican soaps, in 1993 Ricky moved to Los Angeles, California, chasing a dream many Latino actors before him had unsuccessfully pursued—crossover television success in Hollywood. "I really wanted to do something on American TV and they were looking for a Spanish-speaking guy who could sing and act," he told *Star* magazine.

Luckily, while he was in Los Angeles, tapes of his work in Mexican soaps came across the desk of *General Hospital* executive producer Wendy Riche. "Even though they were in Spanish, I connected to him," Riche later said. "He has great charisma and sex appeal."

In the world of daytime soaps, dominated by female viewers, Ricky made an immediate splash, debuting on the

General Hospital's *heartthrob enjoys partying at the 1995 Emmy Awards. Ricky's companion is Lily Melgar, his costar whom he also dated offscreen and who has remained a close friend.*

show by talking a woman out of committing suicide. His character was the mysterious pop star Miguel, who was on the run from an unexplained past in Mexico. As Ricky told *Star:* "Miguel has lots of secrets and one of them is that he used to be a singer in Puerto Rico."

Like all soap operas, the plots on *General Hospital* are full of twists and turns, and Miguel experienced his share of bizarre situations. Despite often hokey story lines, Ricky gave his fans many memorable episodes, including a poignant moment when he sang a ballad in tribute to a dying friend. Ricky used the show as an opportunity to refine his acting skills and become known to the mainstream American public.

The show also introduced him to costar Lily Melgar, whom he dated offscreen for a short time. Their romance was brief, but they remained friends. As Ricky said at the time, "Right now I'm going out with someone who is very jealous. Her name is My Career. [For her] I give up everything."

In his willingness to "give up everything," Ricky opted for other acting roles that took his career on less fortunate paths. He accepted a role in a sitcom, *Barefoot in Paradise,* which suffered from a terrible script and was never televised. Another of his less than memorable roles was as the character Martin in two episodes of a short-lived comedy series called *Getting By.* Although the show included some prominent names—Cindy Williams of *Laverne and Shirley* and Telma Hopkins—in the end it suffered the same fate as most other new shows: It was canceled.

From the time Ricky left Menudo until he graduated from *General Hospital* seems to be the period that defined the new direction his career would take. The success of Ricky's first album led to his second, *Me Amaras* ("You Will Love Me"), which was released in 1993. The album, which won him Best New Latin Artist at the *Billboard* Music Video Awards, was an important step away from his previous tenny-bopper sound.

Though Ricky's singing career was revital-ized, his personal life was in turmoil. The rift between Ricky and his father was still unsettled. It had lingered from the time of Ricky's depar-ture from Menudo, when he chose to live with his mother instead of his father. It wasn't until the death of Ricky's paternal grandfather in 1995 that he took steps to heal the relationship with the senior Martin.

"I couldn't live with [the estrangement] any-more," he told an interviewer. "One of us had to let go of the past and take the first step. He was the father. I knew it had to be me."

Putting his differences with his father behind him took a huge burden off Ricky's shoulders. Lily Melgar recalled, "After he reconciled with his father, Ricky's been the happiest I've ever seen him. He has inner peace."

Ricky's stint on the soap had brought him into millions of American homes. His wildly popular albums were selling around the world. What would be next for the young singer-actor who had worked so hard for success? Ricky would soon find out, when a producer was cap-tured by his charisma and talent and tapped him for a role in a Broadway musical.

LIGHTING UP BROADWAY

O n June 24, 1996, Ricky Martin debuted on Broadway in the role of the French revolutionary Marius in *Les Misérables.* As the house lights dimmed, an audience that included fans, friends, and critics all had the same question: could a young, Spanish-speaking soap opera actor successfully take on one of the most demanding roles on Broadway?

Among those in the packed house that night was Ricky's grandmother, who had put aside her fear of flying to make the event. "We are all calling this a historical occasion because my grandmother hates to fly," Ricky said. "But she said to me, 'Since I don't get to see you on *General Hospital* every day now, I have come to see you in person'— and I'm so glad she did."

Appearing in the musical was a huge step for Ricky. Putting a handsome face on the contrived plots of a soap opera could not begin to compare with the demands of giving a credible performance in this classic Victor Hugo tale of vengeance and sacrifice against the background of a revolutionary uprising in France in the 1830s.

When the bright lights of Broadway beckoned, Ricky left Los Angeles and returned to New York to appear in the smash hit Les Misérables. *Although his run in the musical was short, audiences packed the house to see him, and critics liked his performance.*

For a television actor, who is used to shooting scenes in a studio, to appear onstage before a live audience can be a tremendous step. Unlike television, where if a scene goes wrong it can be reshot, mistakes on the stage cannot be corrected. And theater critics can be most unforgiving. Performing live is much like walking a high wire, but it was a challenge that Ricky was happy to accept.

For Ricky the transition from soaps to musical theater was easier than he had imagined. The producer of *Les Miz* had read an interview Ricky gave in which he had declared his intention of someday appearing on Broadway. As Ricky recounted later, "Richard-Jay Alexander, the executive producer of *Les Miz*, read the interview. He called me and we met. He heard my range, and then told me I had the part."

Alexander certainly had no qualms about Ricky's ability, saying that the young actor-singer had the power "to light up a room that you can't be taught and that money can't buy."

Ricky appeared in *Les Miz* for about three months, and as he learned, theater is a difficult but very satisfying art form. He told *MTV Online:*

> Theatre was great. That's my favorite. That's exactly when you have to really understand the meaning of the word "discipline." It's seven shows a week, and three hours on stage. . . . [It's] kind of addictive and you have to do it again. It is one of the most beautiful things I've done in my life. Just being able to sing, dance, and act and have the audience with you at the same time!

In preparation for the role, Ricky had only 11 days to learn his lines and movements. At the same time, he was also promoting his new album, *A Medio Vivir* ("Halfway Across the Bridge of Life"). Because of his hectic practice and singing schedule, he developed laryngitis, which left him with severely swollen vocal cords. "Imagine four to five days before your Broadway debut and your voice isn't functioning," he said.

His voice did return for opening night, which Ricky called "scary, exhilarating and exhausting" all at the same time. "I felt my adrenaline pumping because the audience that goes to my concerts is already convinced [of my talent] but in the theatre I still have to convince them. It was a real challenge."

Indeed, the idea of a soap-opera star—and moreover, one whose native language was not even English—taking on one of literature's great dramatic works was truly daunting. Knowing that the audience was watching him closely, Ricky said "I was scared to death. Every single scene, from the beginning to the end, I was just dying because the entire theatre was sitting there watching me. Thank God, everyone said to me afterward: 'Oh, you look so comfortable up there,' because I certainly didn't feel it."

Ricky's role in the show was a pivotal move toward becoming a legitimate actor as well as showing audiences that he was serious about his singing. For Ricky, the transition from pop star to soap-opera heartthrob to Broadway singer and actor worked.

Though not the lead, Marius is a highly visible character and is critical to the plot as the young revolutionary who mans the barricades in the streets of Paris during a revolt against the tyranny of the French government. He meets and falls in love with the daughter of the story's leading character, is parted from her, and in the end is reunited with his love. Ricky's role is highly romantic and idealistic, and he sang several emotional numbers during the show.

"Marius is very naïve," Ricky explains. "But he's also been through a lot of stuff that nobody knows about. There is a lot of information in the Victor Hugo novel that isn't in the script, so reading the book was like doing homework. The character goes through a lot of changes. He's a rich kid from the suburbs, and he goes to the city and all of a sudden he's dying of hunger. Then his friend dies in his arms, and he meets some great guys who become his friends, but they all die, too."

Many critics praised Ricky's performance, especially noting his sensitive rendering of the solo "Empty Tables at Empty Chairs." Critics liked the way he moved onstage and were impressed with his romantic presence alongside costar Christeen Michelle Riggs. Although one critic noted that his Spanish accent occasionally peeked through his delivery, his acting was generally good, and audiences gave him many standing ovations.

To prepare for the part, Ricky saw *Les Miz* 27 times. "I wanted to make sure I got it right," he explained to *Soap Opera Digest.* "I'm on stage for nearly three hours because for the first 50 minutes I play a series of characters— a convict, a policeman and a farmer—before I come on as Marius. In the theatre, there's lighting, moving, singing and dancing to worry about, and I wanted to do my homework."

The thrill of being "up on the high wire" was especially appealing to Ricky. As he described it, one of his main pleasures came from "working with incredible performers. I've learned a

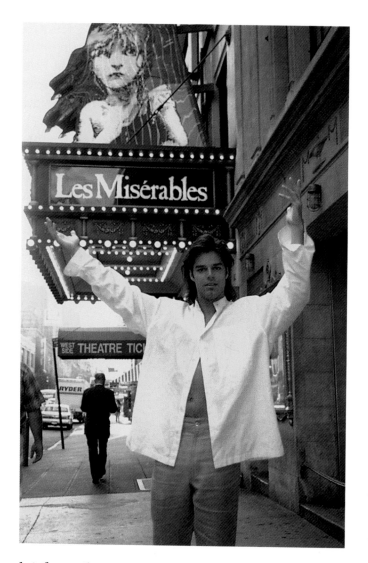

*From acting on a soap
opera to appearing in a
musical was a huge
leap for Ricky. But he
was determined to fulfill
his dream of appearing
on Broadway, and his
hard work paid off
when he excelled in
the role.*

lot from them. And my favorite scene is when
Jean Valjean [the protagonist] is going through
a cathartic moment telling me his life at the
end of the second act."

Although Ricky's move into serious acting
had paid off, at the time it was a major career
risk. He could have failed to win over the critics,
and his performance could have been panned.

For Ricky, the chance to show he could be a

legitimate actor was worth the risk. "I left _GH_ [_General Hospital_] because I had the opportunity to do _Les Misérables_ on Broadway and that was a lifelong dream," he said. "_General Hospital_ was a great experience, but moving back to New York was the right thing to do."

Success on Broadway was one of the brightest moments in Ricky's climb to the top, and his personal life took a backseat to his career. He was still dating Rebecca de Alba off and on, but he had definitely chosen a career over a relationship. If there was any doubt whether his love was acting or singing, he made that clear. "If I have to choose, without a doubt, music is what I love," he said. "A lot of people ask me about acting [in films]. I would love to do acting with the right director, with the right cast, but for me, there's nothing like music."

With the release of _A Medio Vivir_, a more mature Ricky Martin sound was unveiled to the public. Although the Latin beat was present, other musical influences were beginning to emerge. Just as important for his development, Ricky was working with producers who knew him—and who knew what he wanted to say with his music. These included Robi Draco Rosa (Ian Blake in the credits) and KC Porter, who specialized in producing crossover artists.

A Medio Vivir was Ricky's most personal album to date. "Everything that you listen to in this album—that's my life," he explained. "I sat with different composers and told them what I wanted to express, what I was going through at that moment in my life and how I wanted to approach the audience with that album."

Included in the album was the monster hit song "María," which describes a kind of woman Ricky is quite familiar with—one who plays with a guy's mind, first saying yes and then saying no. Apparently Ricky had dated quite a few women like Maria. A remix of "María" became the number-one song in France, Belgium, Australia, and Spain and was also the number-two top-selling international single of 1997.

In addition to recording, Ricky got into films in a roundabout way, singing the theme song "No Importa la Distancia" ("Go the Distance") for the Spanish version of the 1997 Disney animated movie *Hercules*. He was also the voice of the title character. During the same period, moviegoers who saw the Antonio Banderas film *The Mask of Zorro* heard Ricky perform the background music.

With his successful venture on Broadway behind him and a new phase of more personalized music underway, Ricky was delighted with the direction of his career, stating:

> If I get tired of this I will quit. How simple is that? I said to myself a couple of years ago that I was not going to do anything that I was not comfortable with. I will love to do this for a long time, but I mean . . . I don't want to sound egocentric, but it's my well being, you know? Life is too short to be doing something you don't like, so let's take advantage of every moment while we're doing this.

As Ricky finally felt in control of his own destiny, the horizon seemed brighter than ever. At this point there was no turning back.

6

The Cup
Runneth Over

In September 1998, Ricky captured the hearts of viewers worldwide when he sang "La Copa de la Vida" at soccer's World Cup games in France. Standing on the field amidst all the passion and pageantry of the closing ceremonies, Ricky performed with startling dramatic intensity. Singing for viewers in some 87 countries, he rendered parts of the song in Spanish, English, and French and truly captured the spirit and passion of the occasion.

In many ways, Ricky Martin truly embodied the lyrics of the song. Like Ricky's determination and ambition, the song is really all about giving everything you have—win or lose—and putting your best foot forward. The fact that so many viewers related to his performance was a testament not only to Ricky's abilities as a singer but also to himself as an individual.

After he finished, the roar from the audience told him that his performance had struck a chord. "It was a fascinating experience, but I was ready because I had been preparing for more than a month. The audience was really warm, but the first thing I did when I left the stadium was

Ricky performs in New Delhi, India, on his whirlwind 1998 concert tour. As he sang and danced his way from country to country, he attracted crowds of new fans, adding to those millions who already loved him.

to call my mom to check if I had come through clearly at home. She was in tears, so I knew it was a success."

Ricky's appearance at the World Cup was just one of many highlights that year in a whirlwind quest to capture fans across the globe. In a few short months, Ricky's concert tour took him from Japan to Argentina, Spain, France, Greece, Hungary, Belgium, Israel, and Turkey, and then back to France. Carried by the momentum of the single "María," his *Vuelve* album sold more than 950,000 copies in the United States alone.

On continent after continent, the album—produced by KC Porter and his old friend Robi Draco Rosa—attracted scores of new fans and increased respect for the young performer's music. Ricky's plan was to branch out from his Spanish fan base and add new admirers in Latin America, Asia, Europe, and finally the United States. All the pieces were falling into place as he performed one sold-out show after another.

Though his musical career was peaking, Ricky's personal life was still on hold. During most of his career, the one constant in his romantic life has been Rebecca de Alba. Aside from his brief liaison with Lily Melgar, Rebecca remained the "special woman" in Ricky's life. Throughout his career, Rebecca, who is a successful model and television hostess in Mexico, has been the only real public partner that his fans have ever seen.

Although the couple appears publicly, Ricky has always kept his relationship with Rebecca private. "Rebecca is someone very special. I understand that a gentleman doesn't talk about his women and respects them. Why

make public the person you go out with? No."

The hectic nature of their careers has made for a bumpy relationship, but even after break-ups, Ricky always speaks of getting back together. The title song of *Vuelve* sheds some light on Ricky's feelings for his long-time partner. As he explains:

Ricky rehearses with his dancers. Touring demands a large group of backup people and an enormous amount of hard work and preparation.

> The title song on this album came after a break with a very special person in my life. It still hurts sometimes when I sing the gospel chorus, I feel like the stage is sinking under my feet.

At one point, in 1996, Ricky almost asked Rebecca to marry him. He went so far as to buy the ring, but changed his mind at the last minute. His affection and respect for Rebecca endure, however. If he does get married, she

Sony Records presented Ricky with an award to honor his album Vuelve. *Fans snapped up the album, buying more than 950,000 copies in the United States and thousands more worldwide.*

might likely be the one since she has many of the traits he looks for in a woman. "She's so feminine, very sensual, knows how to pamper herself," he says. "I need a woman who really knows how to take care of herself. She has a lot of class, and she's brilliant, which turns me on. Rebecca is a very talented, focused woman who knows what she wants."

When asked by one reporter what appeals to him in women, Ricky responded: "I like the women who have the beautiful skin and big eyes. I like the Latin women, because they have my idiom and my blood; but I would marry a German woman if she can do Latin foods." When asked what physical characteristics he looks for, he replies, "The legs, but what really arrests me is her smell. And if I never see her again I go mad."

When Ricky and Rebecca appeared together at the Grammys, Rebecca spoke as if she were committed to Ricky for the long run. She said she was supporting Ricky in his career and that she was "his woman" and he was "her man." She added, though, that they had no marriage plans at the moment. Although Rebecca and Ricky split again after the Grammys, given the history of their relationship, chances are the flame will be rekindled in the future.

But whoever Ricky chooses to marry, there will always be the conflict within him between the demands of his career and his desire for a stable home life. At some point, Ricky does envision settling down and getting married, contending that "I will have many children. My dream has always been to construct a family.

LIVIN' LA VIDA LOCA

H ow can one explain the incredible success of Ricky Martin? Why have countless other performers been popular abroad but never broken through in the United States? Why, among all the musicians who have started out as teenybopper idols, is Ricky one of the few to go on to even greater success? How did a little boy from Puerto Rico who once performed simple plays for his friends reach the pinnacle of success in the world of pop music? Something about Ricky Martin will not be denied: He has an incredible will to succeed and the discipline to achieve his dreams.

In the history of pop music, few Latin performers have been able to cross over from Latin pop and break through into the American market. Times are changing, however, and Latin performers are entering the scene to capture Anglo audiences. Among them are stars such as Gloria Estefan, whose blend of salsa, pop, and dance has sold millions of records to both Hispanic and Anglo fans. Others in the new generation of Latino singers also include Marc Anthony, Jennifer Lopez, and Enrique

---

Following the 1999 Grammy Awards, Ricky's fame spread like wildfire in the United States. When he appeared on The Tonight Show *with Jay Leno, hordes of fans began lining up the night before for free tickets.*

Iglesias. Of them, Ricky Martin is deemed the hottest new star.

If there is any question about Ricky's overwhelming effect on his fans, passersby only had to watch a scene outside a Tower Records store in New York City. A screaming, scrambling crowd of some 5,000 admirers pushed into the store and jammed the sidewalk to catch a glimpse of their idol or snag his signature on a poster or CD. Many of the lucky ones could be seen leaving the store crying with joy.

In the pop world, Ricky's "Livin' la Vida Loca" was a number-one song. As a single, this first song from his English-language album *Ricky Martin* was played constantly on radio stations around the globe. Upon its release, the single sold 280,000 copies, and the album sold more copies in its first week than that of any artist in 1999. Amazingly, even as fans bought the single, they also bought the album. In addition, "La Copa de la Vida" became a number-one hit in 20 countries, including Turkey, Japan, Mexico, Argentina, Australia, Thailand, and Italy. Fans, it seemed, could not get enough of Ricky Martin.

Ricky continues to oblige his audiences. In the fall of 1999, he kicked off a long-anticipated U.S. tour, which included 15 cities. In an interview with an *MTV News* reporter, he radiated enthusiasm as he described the show he had planned. "You'll have the Latin touch. You'll be dancing a lot in the show, definitely. . . . We're talking an amazing band. People that I've worked with for many years. People who know the meaning of the word fusion. And that's exactly what we want to share with the audience."

Fans who can't get to see Ricky on tour

As the public demanded more and more of Ricky, he became a constant guest on talk shows, where his appearance was sure to raise the ratings. Here he performs on the Late Show with David Letterman.

can content themselves with his MTV video of _Livin' la Vida Loca,_ a swinging four-minute dance party featuring a hip-swiveling Ricky in black leather. According to the producer, "The video is on all day long, and it keeps getting requested." Another music video was released in fall 1999, in which Ricky teamed up with Madonna to do a dynamic performance of their duet "Cuidado con Mi Corazon" ("Be Careful with My Heart").

Ricky's television appearances include stints on *Saturday Night Live* and a live concert on the *Today Show*, which garnered one of the program's highest ratings in 1999. And his commercial, "Come Discover Puerto Rico," in which he promotes tourism, pops up all over American television. Also in 1999, Ricky mounted his first televised concert special on CBS. As a testament to his incredible popularity, advertising rates for the special were said to be as high as they have ever been for such a show.

At the end of the year, Ricky was leading *Billboard*'s year-end charts in all categories. He had won a Grammy and MTV Music Video Awards. He has become the top priority for Columbia Records, where he has a multi-album deal. By the age of 27, Ricky had already sold enough gold and platinum albums to make him the best-selling Latin artist ever.

Like all entertainers, Ricky follows a hectic schedule to keep up with his commitments. He tries to take his work, and his life, one day at a time, and he maintains that prayers and meditations help him keep his feet on the ground. Since Ricky intends to have a career for a long time, he is determined that his life should be as simple as he can make it.

As Ricky's phenomenal success continues, he faces challenges along the way, one of which is defending himself against charges of abandoning his Spanish audience. As he carefully explains, "I will never stop singing in Spanish

—that's who I am—but this was always part of the plan."

He also contends with a persistent rumor that he might be gay. Such gossip may come from the fact that he has scores of gay fans as well as straight admirers. Ricky dismisses such talk as something that has never really mattered to him one way or another. He is not particularly concerned with what others think about his sexuality.

To Ricky, relationships are simply a private matter, and he has no intention of making that part of his private life public. His relationships, whether with women, friends, or his family belong entirely to him. Ricky has said that if people want to know him better, they should watch his performances and listen carefully to his music, through which he expresses himself.

In spite of all his efforts at exposure, Ricky also jealously guards his privacy. He needs to be alone for at least several minutes a day, whether on tour or in his multimillion-dollar home in Miami Beach, so that he can explore his feelings. He has explained that he has to have time to make sure he is making the right decisions about his music and his career.

For Ricky, some of the simple rewards of his success mean the most. These moments come for him when he is standing outside of the glare of the spotlight or with his friends or family. When he has time, he can be seen hosting family barbecues by his pool and performing for those he loves best. Having reconciled with his father, the two now talk at least once a week. His career is skyrocketing and he counts on his family's support to help him deal with his fame.

HILLARY'S FOES ★ TEEN FLICKS ★ DINOSAUR EGGS

Newsweek

www.newsweek.c   July 12, 1999 : $3.50

Latin

How Young Hispanics Are Changing America

U.S.A.

Author Junot Díaz, singer Shakira, boxer Oscar De La Hoya

Mainstream magazines have not ignored the popularity of Ricky Martin. Newsweek's July 12, 1999, issue featured an article about how he and other young Latino performers are changing America's culture.

Ricky's impulse to sing for the simple reason that he enjoys it is exemplified by an incident that occurred when he was appearing in concert in Buenos Aires, Argentina. Plagued by the press and longing for time for himself, he sneaked out of his hotel and took a cab to a small restaurant away from the center of the city. Once there, he sang and danced with the customers and said later that it was the most exciting concert he had done.

Whether Ricky Martin's music is electrifying millions of fans or just entertaining people in a restaurant in Buenos Aires, he can be content with the fact that he has helped open the doors to a new era in Latin music. As he has expressed his philosophy about the effect of his music on his listeners, "I want them to feel free, liberated. I want them to be who they are with my music."

CHRONOLOGY

1971	Born Enrique Martin Morales on December 24 in San Juan, Puerto Rico.
1978	Appears in first television commercial for Orange Crush soda.
1984–89	Joins the boy band Menudo; travels and performs with the band.
1989	Leaves Menudo; moves to New York City.
1991	Signs recording contract with Sony Records.
1992	Moves to Mexico City; appears in Mexican soap opera *Alcanzar una Estrella II;* first solo Spanish-language album, *Ricky Martin,* is released.
1993	Moves to Hollywood, California; second album, *Me Amarás,* is released.
1994	Plays role of Miguel Morez on soap opera *General Hospital;* appears briefly in sitcom *Getting By.*
1995	Third album, *A Medio Vivir,* is released.
1996	Appears as Marius in Broadway production of *Les Misérables.*
1998	Performs "La Copa de la Vida" at the World Cup soccer games in France; record label Sony releases album *Vuelve.*
1999	Performs "La Copa de la Vida" at the Grammy Awards; record label releases English-language version of album *Ricky Martin.*

ACCOMPLISHMENTS

Albums

1992   *Ricky Martin* (Spanish)

1993   *Me Amarás* (You Will Love Me)

1995   *A Medio Vivir* (Halfway Across the Bridge of Life)

1998   *Vuelve* (Come Back)

1999   *Ricky Martin* (English-language debut)

Television

1992–94   *Alcanzar una Estrella II* (in Mexico)

1993–94   *Getting By*

1994–96   *General Hospital*

Theater

1992   *Mamá Ama el Rock* (Mom Loves Rock)

1996   *Les Misérables*

Awards

1990   Heraldo Award (Mexican award) for *Mas que Alcanzar una Estrella*

1993   *Billboard* Award for Best New Latin Artist

1999   Grammy for Best Latin Pop Performance for *Vuelve*
        MTV Video Music Award for Best Dance Video and Best Pop Video for *Livin' la Vida Loca*

FURTHER READING

Furman, Elina. *Ricky Martin.* New York: St Martin's Paperbacks, 1999.

Krulik, Nancy. *Ricky Martin: Rockin' the House!* New York: Pocket Books, 1999.

Marrero, Letisha. *Ricky Martin Livin' la Vida Loca.* New York: Harper Entertainment, 1999.

Marron, Maggie. *Ricky Martin.* New York: Barnes & Noble Books, 1999.

Sparks, Kristin. *Ricky Martin: Livin' la Vida Loca.* New York: Berkley Publishing Group, 1999.

Tracy, Kathleen. *Ricky Martin: Red Hot and on the Rise.* New York: Zebra Books, 1999.

About the Author

MATTHEW NEWMAN loves writing biographies for children. He is a graduate of the University of California at Berkeley. He has authored eight children's books and published adult fiction in *Apalachee Quarterly*. He was the screenwriter for a biographical video, *Handel's Messiah*, and producer of a Spanish-language soap opera for high school students, *La Catrina*. Currently, he is producing a science website for elementary school students. An avid music fan, he once played guitar in a fun but now defunct Chicago-based band, Rant/Chant.

INDEX

Alcanzar una Estrella II ("Reaching for a Star 2"), 30

Alexander, Richard-Jay, 40

A Medio Vivir ("Halfway Across the Bridge of Life") (album), 41, 44-45

Anthony, Marc, 9, 53

CBS television special, 7, 56

Child, Desmond, 9-10

Columbia Records, 56

"Come Discover Puerto Rico" (TV commercial), 56

"Copa de la Vida, La" (single), 8-9, 10-11, 47-48, 54

"Cuidado con Mi Corazon" ("Be Careful with My Heart") (single), 12, 56

Cuidado con Mi Corazon ("Be Careful with My Heart") (video), 56

de Alba, Rebecca, 10, 31, 44, 48-51

Diaz, Edgardo, 22

Estefan, Emilio, 9

Estefan, Gloria, 9, 53

General Hospital, 35-36, 44

Getting By, 36

Grammy Awards, 7, 8-12, 15, 56

Hercules (film), 45

Iglesias, Enrique, 11, 53-54

"Livin' la Vida Loca" (single), 9, 27, 54

Livin' la Vida Loca (video), 12, 55-56

Lopez, Jennifer, 9, 53

Madonna, 12, 14, 56

Mamá Ama el Rock ("Mom Loves Rock"), 30

"María" (single), 44-45, 48

Martin, Enrique (father), 19-20, 21, 28, 37, 57

Martin, Ricky
and American concert tour, 7, 54
birth of, 19
childhood of, 19-20
education of, 20
family of, 19-21, 23, 28, 37, 57
in Hollywood, 35
in Mexico City, 30-31
in Miami Beach, 57
in New York City, 28-30
and trademark phrase, 7, 8, 12

Mask of Zorro, The (film), 45

Mas que Alcanzar una Estrella ("More Than Reaching for a Star"), 31

Me Amaras ("You Will Love Me") (album), 37

Melgar, Lily, 36, 37, 48

Menudo, 8, 9, 18-23, 25-28, 30, 36, 37

Misérables, Les, 39-44

Morales, Nereida (mother), 19, 21, 28, 37, 48

MTV Music Awards, 7, 56

Muñecos del Papel ("Paper Dolls"), 31

"No Importa la Distancia" ("Go the Distance") (single), 45

Porter, KC, 44, 48

Riche, Wendy, 35

Ricky Martin (album, English-language), 54

Ricky Martin (album, Spanish-language), 30, 31

Rosa, Robi Draco, 9, 14, 26-27, 44, 48

Saturday Night Live, 56

Sony Records, 30, 31

Today Show, 56

"Vuelve" ("Return") (single), 49

Vuelve ("Return") (album), 12, 48, 49

World Cup championship, 9, 47-48